By Joel E. Smith, EA, MSA

ISBN: 979-8-218-08787-6
Two Eagles Publishing LLC

PREFACE

On March 11, 2003, at 7:54 AM, I hit a patch of black ice while driving my three young sons to school. Fortunately, none of them were seriously injured. But, in an instant, my life changed. Months in a wheelchair, months on a walker, months with crutches. My wife was working so I was alone during the day. I had recently become involved as a volunteer with some youth not-for-profit (NFP) organizations to be more involved with my two older sons, then seven and nine years old. Other parent volunteers from these organizations checked in on me and brought meals for our family. Soon, other NFPs started helping us out as well. I looked forward to my weekly visit from a member of the Knights of Columbus (I was not a member) who would bring me sandwiches to last the week.

By late July of that year, I had recuperated to the point that, though still using a walker, I was able to get out in the world and even return to work part-time. One night we had guests over to the house. Suddenly one of them noticed smoke rising from our floorboards. This was followed by the smoke detectors going off. From our neighbor's front yard, with me leaning on my walker, we watched our house burn down.

Dealing with the insurance company was nightmarish. The larger organizations do not help unless it is an event that affects communities as a whole.

The outpouring of support in many forms from local nonprofit organizations and the community at large was overwhelming. We likely would not have gotten through the summer without it. A case in point was the Scout family that shared their home with us for two weeks: my wife, myself, and our three young sons. This time was spent searching for a home to rent while ours was being rebuilt. After that we were a family of volunteers, paying it back to the community that had so generously helped us in our time of need. Fortunately for us, family, friends, and small local Nonprofits stepped in again to help us out.

At this point, I desired to be able to volunteer when and where I could from that day on. I have now been involved as a Scout leader for more than 20 years, a volunteer gleaner for the Society of Saint Andrew, and a Board member for the defunct Shenandoah Valley Hockey League. Currently, I am a board member, and a member of the finance committee, for NW Works in Winchester.

In 2012 I took a position with an accounting firm whose primary revenue source was from attestation services for nonprofits and Form 990: Return of Organization Exempt From Income Tax. Until that time, I had no idea such a thing existed. I remember a day one of the CPAs was working with a new client to abate tens of thousands of dollars in penalties due to an incorrectly prepared return. I was instantly hooked. I would rather see worthwhile organizations spend funds on their programs than have to pay the Internal Revenue Service for an incorrect Form 990.

From there I learned about more than just the numbers on the 990. There are many facets of Form 990 that so many organizations do not understand, nor do they realize how these things can apply to them. I have also come to understand how important the various intertwined roles of a nonprofit are. It is my goal to shed some light on these matters and also help them utilize other resources to promote their missions. This book is primarily designed for those with smaller local nonprofit organizations and those thinking about starting one or becoming involved with one. The overall scope of nonprofits, however, is wide enough that others will benefit from it as well.

Acknowledgments

I would like to thank those who both encouraged me and supported me in this endeavor. Those who offered me feedback and insight and made suggestions for improvement I had not even considered. While there were many, the three most impactful were David Burkhardt, CPA, my son Dimitri, and Michael Callahan, CPA. David introduced me to the world of the 990s and was my early mentor. Dimitri offered many of the ideas for improvement and kept up with me on the progress, continuing to provide feedback. Michael prodded and encouraged me when I hit slow periods and without him, I'm not certain it would ever have been completed.

TABLE OF CONTENTS

Chapter 1

What is a Nonprofit?

. There are many terms for nonprofits: charitable organizations, charities, not-for-profit, and philanthropic organizations among others. But there are also associations, clubs, leagues, and other organizations that may be nonprofits. Then there is the Internal Revenue Service (IRS) term: Exempt Organization. For the sake of simplicity, I will refer to Exempt Organizations as nonprofits throughout the book. However, it is important to understand that there is a difference between the terms nonprofit and tax-exempt. Nonprofit status is a state concept whereby corporations are formed for the purpose of benefiting a segment of society, without the specific intent to earn a profit or pass profits on to its members or staff. Tax-exempt is a federal designation meaning the organization is not subject to income taxes on any profits it does make. While 501(c)(3) organizations are fully tax-exempt, not all classifications of nonprofits are.

First, we need to consider what a nonprofit is and what is not a nonprofit. The purpose of a nonprofit is to promote a specific social cause, but the mere act of supporting persons, places, or things does not make a nonprofit. Every nonprofit in the United States starts its journey as a legitimate organization by registering with its respective state, usually as a non-stock corporation. The organization then files the appropriate Form 1023 or Form 1024, as required, with the IRS for tax-exempt status. Many states require a separate registration to solicit contributions. Asking for contributions to support your pet cause, if your organization is not properly registered, could be illegal. Not everyone understands this. I once ran into some people who were soliciting donations for their nonprofit. When asked the name of the organization they bluntly replied, "It's our family nonprofit." Upon pressing them a bit further (had they filed their 1023, could I look them up on Candid GuideStar?) they gave me a blank stare. Finally, one of them responded that they collected donations from people and then passed them on to people they knew who were in need. That does not qualify as a nonprofit. While writing this I spoke with a gentleman who said he 'had' a nonprofit. After questioning him I learned he has run it for several years. Several events have been held to raise money for his cause. I asked for the name of the organization and quickly checked both irs.org and Candid GuideStar but did not find it on either source. When I questioned him further, he said that the nonprofit status with the IRS had just been applied for this year and is pending. He said he didn't break any rules because he never solicited funds. Yet people freely donated funds thinking it was a legitimate charitable organization. When I mentioned this, he said he hadn't considered that aspect. As a tax professional, I have many times had people try to claim charitable deductions for money they had given to friends, neighbors, and family members without understanding these do not qualify as tax-deductible contributions to a qualified charitable organization.

The term 'nonprofit' is a misnomer. It makes it sound as if the organizations do not or cannot make a profit, but this is far from true. It is still a business and needs to be operated like one. It can, and should, make a profit to remain viable, especially to have reserves in times of reduced contributions, grants, or program revenue. Nonprofits and for-profit businesses have similarities in how they report revenues and expenses, but also many differences. And not all nonprofits use the same accounting,

While all charities are nonprofits, not all nonprofits are charities. Charities have a philanthropic purpose and are broadly defined as being established for purposes that are religious, educational, charitable, scientific, literary, testing for public safety, fostering of national or international amateur sports, or prevention of cruelty to animals and children. Charities are created to improve the communities they serve and beyond and can be either public charities or private foundations.

There are many types of nonprofits. Churches are automatically considered to be nonprofits because of their religious nature and do not have to formally apply to the IRS for nonprofit status. Some do, but this means there are two separate entities: the church, and the nonprofit. This involves additional costs to the church, and potential loss of church contributions (Divirgilio, 2015). Churches do have to incorporate as a non-stock charitable organization in their state and obtain an Employer Identification Number (EIN) from the IRS.

Other than churches, the most widely recognized nonprofits are 501(c)(3) organizations. Being a "501(c)(3)" means that a particular nonprofit organization has been approved by the Internal Revenue Service as a tax-exempt, charitable organization meeting one of the purposes stated above. Many people do not realize that donations to political parties or fraternal organizations are not deductible. Only contributions to religious organizations and 501(c)(3) organizations, qualified charities in Canada, Israel, and Mexico, and two types of 501(c)(4) organizations (volunteer fire and rescue departments, and war veterans' organizations) are tax-deductible. Even then, there can be limiting factors. Your deductions may be limited to anywhere from 20% to 60% of your Adjusted Gross Income (AGI) depending on the receiving organization, the type of contribution, and your AGI. Any amounts not allowed in one tax year can be carried forward for five years. Another limiting factor is the value received from any donation. An example is buying Girl Scout cookies. The cookies have value, but they also have a donation factor. Say you spend $5.00 on a box of cookies. A similar box in the grocery store would cost you $2.50. Therefore, only the $2.50 you pay above the value is deductible. Another example would be an event such as a meal or concert. You pay $100 for your event, but the value of the meal is $40 if you bought it directly from the caterer; in this case, the additional $60 is deductible. If you have any questions regarding whether your contribution is deductible or not, ask the recipient organization and refer to IRS Publication 526.

Also well-known are 501(c)(4) organizations which cover civic leagues, local associations of employees, and social welfare organizations. The intent of a civic league is to improve the quality of life in the communities they serve. While this sounds like a charitable 501(c)(3), the difference is that they are membership organizations having 10 or more members. This could be a local service club, veterans post, fraternal society, volunteer fire or rescue group, or otherwise. Examples are Civitan International and Lions Club International

501(c)(6) organizations exist to promote members' business interests. These include Chambers of Commerce, real estate boards, and trade associations. Many may be surprised to learn that trade associations can include sports leagues. The NAACP, NHL, PGA, and the U.S Olympic Committee all fall into this category. The NFL became a nonprofit in 1966 but converted back to a for-profit entity in 2015 for a variety of reasons (Zagorsky, 2015)

Many 501(c)(8) or 501(c)(10) are well-known as fraternal organizations. Among these entities are the Elks Lodge, Freemasons, Knights of Columbus, Moose Lodge, and the Shriners.

Currently, there are 27 types of 501(c) organizations, and another five 501 classifications all treated as tax-exempt entities. A few examples are black lung benefits trusts, cemetery companies, farmers' cooperatives, and mutual insurance company associations (Ensor, 2022).

Now that we have a better understanding of what nonprofits are, and are not, what are the roles referenced by the title of the book? How does this relate to you, the reader? We all play many roles in life, and when we accept that role, we accept the responsibilities that go with those roles. An actor has a responsibility to play a part to the best of their capability and make it believable to the audience. Parents have the responsibility to raise their children into someone who functions well in society, to feed them, protect them and shelter them until they can do so on their own. Teachers have a responsibility to teach their students. Schools have a responsibility to hire qualified teachers and staff and present a good learning environment.

There are tiers within the roles and co-existence between the roles. Using schools as an example, the local constituents elect the school board. The local government funds the schools. Principals, coaches, medical staff, and custodial staff must be hired, and transportation needs to be arranged. Students have the responsibility to come to school, get their homework done, and follow the school rules. Parents or guardians need to make certain their children or wards are doing the aforementioned duties. As you can see, there are multiple intertwining duties.

It is the same with nonprofits. They may be supported financially by businesses, governments, individuals, membership dues, program fees, and even other nonprofits. There are regulations, staff, and community involvement. The roles include the governing board, officers, advisors, consultants, staff, volunteers, governmental agencies, communities, businesses, contributors, monitoring organizations, other organizations, and something that ties them all together, the 990 and attestation services.

Chapter 2

The 990: The Basics and the Role

The Basics

The 990 is not a tax return per se (except for the 990-T) but rather a "Return of Organization Exempt From Income Tax." Essentially it is an informational return providing insight into the organization to the IRS, other government authorities, lenders, people within the organization, and the public. Why is it important? First, because it is a public document. It is available online at irs.gov and GuideStar.org as well as other websites, If someone requests a copy of the 990 from the organization, it is required to be made available. There is even a question on the 990 that asks how it is made available. There are many other reasons as well, among them: 1) It provides financial information that can show stewardship of the public support. 2) Compliance with other Federal laws such as payroll and information reporting and foreign financial activities and accounts. 3) Demonstrating the organization is continuing to serve the mission for which it was granted tax-exempt status by reporting accomplishments and activities for the preceding year. I considered writing a separate book just about the importance of the 990. But it is so relevant to understanding nonprofits and the diligence with which various roles are played out, that I felt it necessary to at least briefly cover it in this book. Overall, the 990 itself plays a role in the health of a nonprofit organization by shedding light on its inner workings.

This chapter is not intended to instruct someone on how to properly prepare a 990, though it will give the reader insight into some of the complexities. Rather it provides insight into what the 990s are, why they matter, and pitfalls to be aware of. We will focus primarily on the full 990 rather than the 990-EZ, or 990-N. Filing a 990-EZ, or 990-N may technically be the correct form for your organization, and certainly, they are easier and less costly to prepare, but they are not necessarily the best forms to file. If you want to grow the organization and maximize its exposure, going to the next form up can help achieve those goals. Remember, this book isn't just for professionals but for beginners and the uninitiated as well. Despite having been personally involved with half a dozen nonprofits over more than two decades, and having prepared tax returns for a while, it wasn't until 10 years ago that I learned anything about the 990 or had even heard of it. There is also the 990-PF for private foundations and there are no short versions of this form.

The number of nonprofits varies year by year, though the number has averaged about 1.8 million annually for about the last decade. The IRS database provides information on the number of filings and the type of each filing by month for each year. Included in the database are the names of each organization and the date the return was filed. In 2017 approximately 1.53 million 990s were filed. Of those, about 1.2 million were 501(c)(3) or (c)(4) organizations, and only about 300,000 filed 990s or the 990-EZ, with the remainder being the 990-N, PF, or other formats. This number can fluctuate substantially from year to year. Not just because of new organizations forming and applying for exempt status, or others terminating their activities. However, these aren't the only reasons. For example, for most exempt organizations it is required and failure to file it for three consecutive years will result in automatic revocation of tax-exempt status. From 2010 to 2017 the IRS revoked the status of 760,000 organizations. While the entities can get their status reinstated, during that same 2010-to-2017-time frame only about 100,000 did so (Wyland, 2018).

Remember that most churches do not have to file a 990. Certain schools associated with religious organizations and some governmental and political organizations are also not required to file a 990. Most nonprofits file the 990-N, also called the e-Postcard. Generally, an organization whose annual gross receipts are $50,000 or less can file this type of return. There are some exceptions, so make certain to be aware of these if your organization is generally in the $50,000 or less range. One exception is if it has assets of $500,000 or more it would be required to file a complete 990. The information needed for this 990 is basic: the name, EIN, address of the nonprofit, and the name and address of the officer responsible for the filing.

For those organizations that exceed $50,000 in annual revenues, if the revenue for any year is under $200,000 and the assets are under $500,000, they can generally file the 990-EZ. Of course, there are exceptions. If your nonprofit meets the revenue and asset qualifications for the 990-EZ but falls under one of the following examples, the organization will be required to file a full 990:

- A sponsoring organization of one or more donor-advised funds.

- A controlling organization is described in Internal Revenue Code (IRC) Section 512(b)(13).

- An organization that operates one or more hospital facilities.

- A nonprofit health insurance issuer described in IRC Section 501(c)(29).

- A central or parent organization filing a group return on behalf of subordinate organizations under a group exemption.

Further, any private foundation is required to file a 990-PF regardless of revenue or asset amounts.

Once the organization hits revenues of $200,000, assets of $500,000, or any of the exceptions (other than the 990-PF) it is required to file the full 990. There are still more exceptions: a Section 501(d) religious and apostolic organization files Form 1065, a U.S. Return of Partnership, and a nonprofit Homeowner's Association files a Form 1120-H.

As you can see, there are many types of nonprofits and variations of the 990. You need to make certain the correct format is being filed for your organization. I have seen nonprofits that were mislabeled. Sometimes their activities, or their levels of contributions, can cause unintended changes. An example would be an organization that the IRS reclassifies as a private foundation due to the contributions coming primarily from a single individual, corporation, or family.

Nonprofits are required to file their 990s annually under Internal Revenue Code (IRC) Section 6033, which also lists the various filing exemptions. It used to be they could be prepared by hand and mailed in. I have seen many in the past that were prepared this way. As of August 1, 2021, this is no longer the case. All forms of the 990, except the 990-T, must now be filed electronically. As of May 2022, e-filing was still not possible for the 990-T, but the IRS indicated they expected this to be resolved soon.

The standard 990 is 12 pages long, but there are 16 Schedules that may need to be attached depending on the organization's activities and type. All 990s and 990-EZs are required to have at least one of those Schedules attached. In addition, some states have filing requirements. California is the only state that currently has a state version of the 990, but many require filings such as annual solicitation filings, annual reports, or financial reports, or require a copy of the Federal 990 to be filed with the state (State Filing Requirements for Nonprofits, 2022).

Penalties for not filing the required version of the 990, or filing it late, can be harsh, costing the organization up to $105 per day, with a maximum of $54,500. Should the situation not be resolved within the time allotted by the IRS, penalties may also be assessed against the person within the organization deemed to be responsible for the filing at a rate of $10 per day up to $5,000. It isn't enough just to get it filed. The IRS considers any 990 that is inaccurate or incomplete to have not been filed. Understand, if your organization files a 990 that the IRS deems to be incomplete or inaccurate, their position is that it wasn't filed. It would then be considered late, and penalties will be assessed. An interesting thing is that a nonprofit that filers the 990-N can skip filing for two years as long as they file the return for the third year there are no penalties for the missed filings. I have personally prepared over 100 990s, and I have reviewed 100s more. Of the ones I have reviewed, I would estimate that about 20% were well prepared, and often the mistakes are so obvious that nearly anyone would notice them. Because of this, you should make certain to choose the preparer wisely. They should be licensed (CPA, EA, Tax Attorney), and have experience preparing 990s. All three of these professionals are required to take annual continuing education, including ethics as one of the topics of study.

Many nonprofits have an annual review or audit of their financial statements prepared by a CPA firm. It would seem that having them also prepare the 990 because of their knowledge of the finances is a good idea. However, this is not necessarily the case. Depending on the size of the firm, the same people that worked on the review or audit may also prepare the 990. This means they are reviewing their own work. An independent pair of eyes may notice errors that have been overlooked. Auditors also work using the premise of materiality. This means the audited financials may have misclassified something by $1,000s or $10,000s but because it is below what is considered a material amount, the auditor ignores it (Accountinguide, 2022). A $10,000 mistake on the 990, if the same figures are used, would certainly be considered inaccurate. Finally, I have often compared CPAs (and EAs and Tax Attorneys) to being like doctors. A podiatrist and a brain surgeon are both doctors, but I wouldn't want my podiatrist performing my brain surgery. The auditor and/or their firm may be excellent at auditing, but that doesn't necessarily mean they are well-versed in 990 preparations. Whoever prepares it, you should inquire not only about their level of experience but also about their training and if they keep abreast of changes to the 990 and any regulatory changes. The last major overhaul of the 990 was in 2008, but the IRS makes changes on average every two years, and other changes, such as e-filing requirement updates, can happen anytime.

The Role of the 990

Simply put, the 990 is a window into the soul of your nonprofit organization, more so than public events or your website. Events have that feel-good atmosphere but do not show the inner workings or how the funds received are dispersed. Your website can be glossed over highlighting the best of what the organization does and who's involved. However, the lack of a 990 can be as telling as the 990 itself. Unless your organization is one that is exempt from filing the 990, a lack of one may indicate you are either not a legitimate exempt organization or were one but have had your tax-exempt status suspended by the IRS.

People will look at the 990 and at least partially form their opinion on the organization and possibly to some degree on you and other people involved with the organization based on what they read in it. This is especially true when reviewed by those not personally familiar with the organization. It is a public document, meaning anyone can look at it. This includes advisors, banks and creditors, board members, businesses, communities, contributors including foundations and supporting organizations, employees, grantors, the media, volunteers, and potential persons or members of any of these. Also, monitoring and regulatory agencies including the IRS and relevant states will review them. This just gave you an overview of nearly every entity with a role to play in your organization, and they are all tied together through the 990. As mentioned in the previous chapter, it is easily available online, and your organization is required to provide a copy if requested.

Contained in the 12 pages, and the various schedules, are insights into what your organization does, and how well it does it. The 990 instructions actually say that your 990 should tell a story about your organization in Part III: Statement of Program Service Accomplishments. Providing details about your nonprofit's activities, goals and successes can lead to better public perception and increased contributions. Consider the following two statements, which sounds better, and which would you rather contribute to:

1) We get stray animals off the streets.

2) It's estimated there are 10,000 stray cats and dogs living in our community. Many are lost pets in danger of becoming feral and posing risks to our community. In 2021 our organization captured 1,372 of these animals.

> We were able to reunite 143 of them with their owners. The remainder were cleaned up, treated for health issues, and placed in either new homes, foster homes, or with other organizations that work to find new owners for them. Our goal is to make certain no dog or cat in our community is wanting of a good home.

Would it surprise you to learn these are the same organization? The first is an actual description from an animal shelter. The second is what it could look like. The first two pages of the 990 (Parts I through III) give a summary of organizational activities, mission, and accomplishments. Your 990 preparer or another advisor can offer guidance on how to improve the presentation.

The entire 990 tells your organization's story: including how well it manages funds, its governance, and meeting regulatory requirements. While each level of 990 preparation is more complex, and therefore more costly to have prepared, it is worth considering going up a step for a nonprofit that normally files the 990-N or 990-EZ as more information is made available which may garner more attention and activity.

Chapter 3

Governing Board and Officers

As a preparer of the 990s, I used to ask organizations for a list of their officers and directors for the year. Often, I would receive a list of 25 to 40 directors. I had to start specifying 'voting members of the governing board.' Your organization may have many divisional directors and they may have a seat at the table during board meetings, but the distinction between these directors and those with voting rights is important. Only those with voting rights are members of the governing board. Determining who is, or is not, an officer of the organization is equally as important though not necessarily as straightforward. Part of this is determined through the organization's basic governing documents, which are: Form 1023 or 1024 filed with the IRS when forming your nonprofit, the Articles of Incorporation, and the Bylaws. Just like the 990, the 1023 or 1024 is considered a public document and has to be made available if requested. It's amazing how many nonprofits I have asked to provide a copy and they didn't have it. It seems once it was filed, they figured it wasn't important anymore or they just forgot about it.

The Bylaws will set the number of voting members of the governing board (or in some cases trustees) and list the required officers (minimum of President, Secretary, and Treasurer). A question on the 990 concerning governance is whether or not there were any changes to any of the governing documents. An organization whose Bylaws say there should be 10 to 12 voting members of the governing board that decides to change that number needs to remember to amend its Bylaws and answer yes to that question.

The 990 lists all persons who filled the position of a voting member of the board (***hereafter called board members***), even if only for one day during the reporting year. Another question asks how many voting members there were at the end of the year. This confuses some people as there may be one number listed in the section that names all such persons for the year, and a different number for the end-of-the-year amount. A knowledgeable preparer will know how to reconcile this on your 990.

You will also need to report the number of board members that are independent. There are many rules determining independence but, in general, any compensation for any services other than as a board member, any compensation of family members, or financial interest in a business from which the organization obtains products or services, will deem the board member to not be independent. This could potentially translate into a conflict of interest. The involved board member should recuse themselves from any discussion around these matters.

As stated, your Bylaws require a President, Secretary, and Treasurer, and you may have added a few more, such as CEO, CFO, Vice President of Marketing, et cetera. A determination could be made between ‘board officers’ meaning those who are generally board members as well and those who are not. Board officers would be the president or CEO, the Secretary and Treasurer, and occasionally the Executive Director. Just like with the voting members of the governing board, every one of the officers has to be listed on the annual 990. I worked with one organization whose person in charge of finance did not want to have his name appear on a public document and went out of his way to have a title that did not fit any prescribed officer positions. Apparently, he was not alone as the IRS recently changed the rules to make certain people such as him are listed. In addition to those officers listed as required in the bylaws, the IRS considers three other positions to be de facto officers. Whoever runs the day-to-day operations or is responsible for implementing the decisions of the governing board, regardless of their title (though often the Executive Director), is considered to be an officer. The person responsible for managing the organization's finances is an officer. And the person responsible for signing the 990 is considered to be an officer. Finally, if ultimate responsibility resides with two or more individuals (for example, co-presidents or co-treasurers), who can exercise such responsibility in concert or individually, then treat all such individuals as officers. It used to be that any individual who exercised control over any unit of the organization that accounted for 10% or more of the organization's activities was considered an officer. That has been removed, and the primary financial person has been added. Not only does the preparer of the 990 need to be aware of changes such as this, but so should the governing board.

Who is in charge of the organization? It should be the governing board, and they should be passing on decisions to the Executive Director or whoever is running the organization on a daily basis, Too often, the Chairman of the Board or CEO is heading up the governing board and running the operations, or the Executive Director is running the show and instructing the governing board what is needed with little input or oversight from them.

A few years ago, I represented the accounting firm I was employed by at the Non-Profit Council of the Prince William County, Virginia Chamber of Commerce. It was astounding to me that many of the board members and officers representing many of the nonprofits had no clear idea of what was expected of them, what their obligations were, or their potential liabilities.

Let's delve into the duties and roles of these people. One of the primary roles of the governing board is to determine policies and procedures, and how they are monitored. This includes the typical policies of hiring and termination, employee benefits, training required by staff and or volunteers, dissemination of information to the media, and hours of operation. Of course, nonprofits will also need policies surrounding program services or member benefits depending on the type of organization. However, one thing that may not initially come to mind is the segregation of duties. The idea is to reduce the amount of control any one person has over any particular process, especially if financially related. As an example, one person might approve and set up new vendors in the system, but another person has to review invoices and approve the payment. This prevents the first person from creating a fake vendor and writing themself a check. The organization can also implement dual custody, which is where two people are assigned to each step. One person counting cash receipts could easily take some of that money, but having another person also count it reduces this risk because the amounts should be equal.

Segregation of duties is something all businesses should practice, but it is vitally important for nonprofit organizations. If your nonprofit is having an annual audit conducted, segregation of duties processes and monitoring are key components of the risk assessment. Issues resulting from little or no separation of duties, or poor oversight, may be found in an audit and may impact grants or contributions. Fraud in a for-profit company is bad enough, and the person responsible could face jail time. But with a nonprofit, the entity is run with public funds. It is a betrayal of public trust, and it could endanger the organization's tax-exempt status. Most nonprofits are subject to the rules against private inurement, which basically means any person having a close relationship with, or substantial control over the entity, unduly benefits from the organization either directly or indirectly. Consider that a nonprofit CEO could have his son hired for the summer as an intern, and the organization pays his son a starting rate 25% higher than the standard rate for summer interns. That is an indirect benefit, and the CEO certainly has substantial control. Private inurement is also called excess benefit transactions, though there can be a distinction between them. For one thing, the excess benefit transaction rules only apply to organizations that have been a 501(c)(3) or501(c)(4) at any time during the previous five years. IRC Section 4958 covers excess benefit transactions and is more complex than ‘simple’ private inurement (Fortenberry, 2022). Penalties for excess benefit transactions can apply to the person receiving them, the organization, and any management that knew about the transactions. It is the duty of the governing board to ensure public trust and safeguard the continuance of the organization.

The board members have legal responsibilities, or fiduciary duties, including those of care, loyalty, and obedience.

The duty of care means that each member must act in a manner showing care for the organization. They have to attend meetings, make prudent decisions, and it is their responsibility to remain informed. They have to exhibit honesty and good faith and take actions believed to be in the best interests of the organization. Such decisions must include reasonable inquiry. They may be protected from personal liability for actions made in poor judgment, as long as they can demonstrate the action was taken with due care and in good faith.

An engaged board will have proper governance in place, will actively monitor adherence to policies, and have a good understanding of what the policies are and should accomplish. They should also understand how to implement effective monitoring.

The duty of loyalty means that board members or officers are expected to be interested in what is good for the organization and not their own interests. Part of this is the corporate opportunities doctrine. This states that a board member can be in a similar line of work as the nonprofit. However, they cannot appropriate for themselves an idea, investment, project, prospect, or any other opportunity that may be in the best interest of the organization, unless and until such time that the organization has considered and rejected said opportunity. Additionally, the use of the organization's assets for personal use, or self-inurement, is disloyal to the nonprofit. While it is not illegal for the board members to have business transactions with the nonprofit, they cannot do so for the purpose of realizing undue gains. Examples would be offering the same services to the nonprofit at a higher cost than what would be charged to other businesses or providing a lesser product for the same or higher cost. This is not only unethical, but if the self-dealing is found to benefit any individual in the amount of $5,000 or more, it is also illegal. Some of the policies asked about on the 990 are to prevent things such as this from happening and to bring them to light if they do occur.

The duty of obedience is the board members' duty to keep the organization on track. It must stick to its mission, which cannot simply be changed because the governing board decides to do so. To do so can jeopardize your nonprofit or tax-exempt status or both. The organization that wishes to amend its mission statement must first ascertain that the new mission still meets the requirements for tax-exempt status within its designation

(501(c)(3), (c)(4), et cetera). They must then notify the IRS, and also their contributors, If they have members the members must be notified as well (Price, 2018). The organization can add or remove services, but this must be reported on the 990 and if the changes are significant, the IRS will need to be notified. The Articles of Incorporation and the Bylaws may need to be amended in either situation. The amended Articles of Incorporation would need to be submitted to the state. It used to be that the amended Articles of Incorporation and Bylaws would need to be submitted to the IRS but currently, the organization needs to provide a detailed description of any changes on Schedule O. The governing board is legally responsible for all of this, as well as making decisions that positively influence the organization, such as choosing a new CEO or Executive Director, how it carries out its mission, and its public presence.

Virtually every state has rules in place that state that a non-functioning board is a reason for the state attorney general to cause involuntary closure of the organization because it has no guidance or accountability. Several factors are considered, including approving budgets, reviewing annual reports, reviewing, and approving major gifts, major asset transactions, major borrowing, substantial changes to services, and discharging and replacing members for reasons set forth in the Bylaws. A non-functioning board member who needs to be replaced is one who displays one or more of the following attributes: not attending meetings regularly, reviewing agendas and relevant information prior to the meetings, does not share their expertise during meetings, or speaks badly about the organization or those associated with it inside or outside of the organization (Bryce, 2017).

Another reason for strong governance policies and an actively engaged board is the prevention of Founders

Syndrome. This is when a board member and/or officer has excessive and or unchecked control over the organization. Usually, this is a founder who started the organization surrounded by like-minded people to be able to quickly get things going. These people may be friends, relatives, coworkers, or anyone with whom they are familiar. But as people leave or difficulties arise there can be clashes, especially if new board members have differing opinions, speak up, and are brushed off. They may become discouraged and leave, creating turnover and turmoil. Staff and volunteers may also become disaffected. In these cases, it must be remembered that the board, not any individual, is responsible for the organization. There should be clear rules in the Bylaws on dealing with any member who does not follow the directions of the overall board (Founder's Syndrome, 2016). I have witnessed this firsthand, even hearing people say: 'my nonprofit' or 'I own a nonprofit.'

Other problems may also arise, and it does not always have to be a founder or a newer organization. Anyone with excessive and or unchecked control is an example of Founders Syndrome. In an infamous example, the Smithsonian suffered from a case of it in the mid-2000s which resulted in fiscal irresponsibility, an audit by the Inspector General, and scrutiny from both Congress and the IRS. In 2000, Lawrence M Small, a businessman, was hired to head the Smithsonian. His supporters will tell you he used his contacts and business acumen to secure large donations and expand the Smithsonian. Under his tenure, the National Museum of the American Indian and the Udvar-Hazy Center of the National Air and Space Museum were opened. As the Smithsonian is funded largely by Congress, he gave them a resolute picture of declining visitor-ship, and the infrastructure changes needed to turn things around. However, other sources report there were issues from the start of his tenure. In the first two years that he helmed the Smithsonian, seven museum directors resigned. He was also investigated twice for illegal possession of artifacts in his personal collection that he had featured in the Smithsonian magazine (Lawrence M Small "Crisis at the Smithsonian", 2002). The problems compounded over the next few years. After a Smithsonian audit in 2007 uncovered unauthorized expenses, and authorized expenses were subsequently deemed excessive and questionable, Congress took action to freeze the Smithsonian budget and add some additional oversight. Two days after the budgetary amendment was passed, Mr. Small resigned (Michael I Sanders, 2017).

There are symptoms to watch for, policies that can be put into place to prevent such occurrences, and measures that can be taken to resolve the situation should it arise. It is well worth learning more and consulting with someone to prevent this from befalling your organization.

The governing board is responsible for reviewing the 990 and ensuring its accuracy. They should consider how it can provide additional information and portray them in a better light, by exhibiting better governance and transparency. Past officers and directors may simply wish to keep up with the organization or may have a personal reason. If they expect deferred compensation, they may want to check the organization's financials for strength and see how deferred compensation is being reported. Potential officers and directors may review the 990 for all the aforementioned reasons before deciding to join the organization.

The Organization's Duties to the Board Members and Officers

As the board members and officers have a duty to the nonprofit, the nonprofit has a duty to them. Those within the organization tasked with carrying out the orders of the board, or for gathering and providing information to the board, are to be expected to perform these duties with due care. Being properly informed, so they can make the best possible decision, is the organization's duty of care to them.

There is also a duty of loyalty from the organization to those entrusted with its care. They should expect that the organization is forthright with them and does not expose them to personal or professional risks, even if forewarned such risks might be present. Also, that all information provided to them, related to the organization or their role in it, is accurate, clearly stated, complete and relevant.

Stewards of the organization should expect clear policies detailing the organization's expectations of them, generally in the form of a handbook or manual, copies of or access to the Articles of Incorporation, Bylaws, and any other governing documents. When onboarding, they should receive training and orientation. And they should be given a list of advisors and access to them.

These are not just sound policies; in some states, they may be required by law. For example, the aforementioned policies are some of the requirements from the *Guidebook for New Hampshire Charitable Organizations* (GUIDEBOOK FOR NEW HAMPSHIRE CHARITABLE ORGANIZATIONS, 2022). While some states have legal requirements, other states offer no protection at all.

Without protective measures, board members may be sued by other members, employees, governments, volunteers, or other parties. The organization can take steps to protect them by making certain they have the most up-to-date and accurate information for decision-making, by properly documenting all meetings and decisions, and through liability insurance..

Chapter 4

Service Providers

In addition to board members and officers, you may have employees and volunteers, advisors, and consultants. Officers may be employees or volunteers. Advisors may be volunteers or paid consultants. Anyone who is not compensated by the organization is considered to be a volunteer. This generally means most, or all of the board members are volunteers. The 990 reports the number of volunteers. When I review a 990 and see there are uncompensated board members, yet the number of volunteers reported is zero, I have discovered one error and wonder how many more there may be. I have witnessed this far too often.

With volunteers for your organization some considerations are: how do you get them, do you train them, if so, how do you train them, and when and how do you let them go? Many organizations are dependent on volunteers and may have more than one level of volunteers. The Society of St. Andrew is a nonprofit based in Virginia that has a national presence in helping provide food to the needy largely by gleaning leftover farm crops at the end of growing seasons. The organization has volunteer board members and officers. Then there are various roles played by other volunteers such as gleaning field supervisors and gleaners. They also look for drivers to transport food, fundraisers, administrative support, and more. The gleaning shows at least three levels as the board members and officers are overseeing gleaning field supervisors who oversee gleaners and also drivers. The drivers take the produce to soup kitchens, food pantries, homeless shelters, or anywhere that provides food to those in need. Often, the volunteer gleaners are volunteers with other organizations such as various youth groups. The recipient organizations are often staffed by volunteers. This ties into the role of nonprofits in their communities. In the 15 years that I had the pleasure of volunteering with this organization, I filled more than one role, so I understand firsthand what a valuable organization it is. I also understand the complexity of the different activity levels and the interactions between this nonprofit's activities in my area, community businesses, other local organizations, and individual volunteers.

Nonprofits owe it to their volunteers to guide them and protect them. They want simple sign-up and onboarding processes. They should be informed, and in clear detail, of their roles and responsibilities. Posting activities and responsibilities for each defined role on your website and other postings sets expectations in advance and helps prevent any confusion. Volunteers also need to be trained on how to perform their duties. There are different levels and methods of training, but the goal should be to ensure you have happy, motivated, and capable people to help your organization and to facilitate their growth as well.

There should be open lines of communication, so they are comfortable asking questions. They need you to communicate with them. Too little and they may feel lost or unappreciated. Too much can make them feel confused and overwhelmed. They should be notified of any changes quickly and concisely. And they should clearly understand what they are not allowed to do and the repercussions of doing a forbidden act.

People have different motivations for wanting to volunteer but one thing most have in common is that they generally believe in the mission. Utilizing their skills can make them feel appreciated and empowered. They may gain other knowledge or learn new skill sets that they otherwise would not have had the opportunity to learn.

There can also be more tangible benefits. Volunteers for sporting events, or those assisting with fundraisers featuring celebrities or musical performances, have the opportunity to witness something they may not otherwise be able to attend.

For many nonprofits, volunteers are the face of the organization as they are the ones clients may most often interact with. If they are not properly trained, and if there are no checks and balances to monitor their activities, there can be negative consequences. Any breakdown in adhering to policies, clearly communicating rules and expectations, reporting violations, and enforcing all of these, are potential bad publicity for and or legal actions against your organization. A good risk management program will have proper insurance and a strong risk prevention program in place to protect both the nonprofit and the volunteers. There are several risks associated with volunteers such as personal injury to a program recipient, allegations of abuse, and director's oversight.

As a Boy Scout leader, I have had youth protection training (every two years), basic adult leader training, outdoor (camping/hiking) training, and committee training. As our unit is chartered by a Catholic organization, I have had Virtus training. They also ran a background check on me. Yet there are negative stories about Scout leaders who abused their positions and took advantage of the youth in their care. Scout leaders are not alone in this regard and abuses can come from employees and volunteers alike. It can happen anytime the clientele is vulnerable. As one example, in June 2022, a man who was a director and teacher at a Florida performing arts center was arrested for sexual misconduct with four underage teen-aged girls (Pikora, 2022).

Of course, most volunteers provide services without ever having an issue. Many are heroic in their actions. Consider volunteer firefighters rushing into a burning building to save someone or rescue workers in a natural disaster where conditions may be unsanitary and structures unsafe. Others are heroes to those they assist even if there is no danger involved. A Moment of Magic is a nonprofit foundation with chapters and volunteers in 16 locations. The volunteers are college-age students who dress up as superheroes and princesses to visit and brighten the lives of critically ill children. For these children, the volunteers are heroes, figuratively and literally, as they bring joy to these children (DiPaulo, 2019).

Many of the factors for volunteers apply to employees as well. Anyone compensated for their services may be deemed an employee or contractor, so be careful about compensating volunteers, even with gifts unless small and of minimal monetary value. Employees should also be vetted, trained, and have oversight. They should have concise descriptions of their position, job duties, and be aware of all organizational policies affecting them. Some employees, by virtue of their job description and their activities, may be deemed to be officers and they will be under more scrutiny from various sources, especially as they will be identified on the 990. Those being compensated above a certain threshold will also be listed. The organization should also be aware of what constitutes an employee versus a contractor if they have paid contractors. Paid contractors compensated in excess of $100,000 may also have to be reported on the 990.

You may have advisors and/or consultants. Advisors will be non-compensated volunteers, that are part of one or more committees within your organization. Unless your organization's policies prohibit it, there is no rule that committee members must be staff or board members. Generally, these advisors will be employed in or retired from, a field where you could use insight not found within the organization: Examples are accountants, bankers, and financial advisors. They are there because you requested their advice, and their input will be limited to the committee meetings. They may also be providing services to the organization. If this is the case, consider them wisely. Some banks offer special rates and services to nonprofits. There are specialized insurance policies for nonprofits. And of course, nonprofit accounting can be substantially different from that of for-profit businesses. If you seek advice from these fields or others, and the advisors are employed in that field, you should consider those that cater to nonprofits.

Paid consultants may reach out to you or you may seek them out. When they contact you, it may be to provide consulting services for an area you were not even aware of or did not fully understand. They may have a particular area of expertise such as fundraising campaigns or website design. It may be broader such as marketing which could include fundraising campaigns, web presence, and community joint ventures. You may think you don't have the budget for a knowledgeable consultant. However, the cost of hiring one could, and should, either save you more than you spend or generate more revenue than you spend. I once heard consultants described as those who con you out of your money while insulting the way you operate your business. While this is not true of consultants in general, there are those who may not be effective or are more interested in billing you than helping you. More than once I have observed nonprofits that spent substantially more on a fundraising campaign than they realized from it in contributions. Choose your consultants wisely and conduct due diligence on them. Do they work for a firm with experience with, and a reputation for, working with nonprofits, or have their own established practice? What are their references? Do they hold any certifications, and are those meaningful and relevant to what you are looking for?

The adage goes: “You get what you pay for.” But sometimes it should be ‘you get what you don’t pay for.’ Understandably, many nonprofits want to keep expenses down, especially smaller ones with tight budgets. However, would you rather pay $500 more for your 990 or pay $5,000 in penalties, plus miss out on potential donations and qualified staff or volunteers because of a poorly prepared one? Would you rather pay a few thousand dollars to initiate a training program or much more from lawsuits, or lose revenue because of poorly trained staff and volunteers?

Some college programs require students to intern for nonprofits. Others may independently apply to intern with your organization. These can be paid or unpaid positions. They may develop into regular employees, and or become ambassadors for you through their shared opinion in future years. You can help shape the future of the interns, and get a fresh perspective on your nonprofit from their viewpoint,

It is your role to engage the best people for your organization, educate them, empower them, and protect them. It is also your duty to protect those you serve, and those you employ, contract, or have as volunteers. In addition to vetting, training, and effective communication, make certain there are signed confidentiality agreements. Be sure to thank them for their contributions.

Chapter 5

Community Duty

A nonprofit's impact on a community will depend in part on the type of entity. A 501(c)(3) offering food, housing, or other social services may have a greater impact on the citizens than other types of entities such as political organizations or voluntary employees' beneficiary associations, but all of them benefit someone. Society depends on these organizations to fill gaps in society, assist those in need, foster education, mental and emotional well-being, business development, and a voice in government among others. If the only fire department in your community is a volunteer fire department, the loss of it through a lack of support or poor management would be devastating to that community.

It's easy to recognize the impact of nonprofits when they benefit you or those you know in the aforementioned ways. But again, all of us are impacted by them in some way. If you use the library, the books may have been donated. The park you visit may have benches, gardens, or trails built by organizations. Often these are Eagle Scout projects. You or a family member may have been born in a non-profit hospital. The server waiting on you in your favorite restaurant may be there only because of the assistance of a nonprofit. The effects are far-reaching.

Because of my experience with and passion for nonprofits I am aware of many local organizations that others are not familiar with. I have people occasionally contact me to ask where to go for help with things. The small city where I live is graced with organizations such as a homeless shelter, food pantries, an orphanage, a youth center, animal rescue, an alcohol and drug rehab center, suicide prevention, a domestic abuse center, and myriad more. I am on the board of a local nonprofit that assists those with disabilities or other employment barriers with learning skills and finding meaningful employment.

The role of the nonprofits here is to fill these needs that cannot be met elsewhere, whether through family, friends, employers, government, or otherwise. It may be essential needs such as food, clothing, shelter, or protection. There is emotional and spiritual support in the form of crisis centers and religious organizations and public services like volunteer fire departments or rescue squads.

They may help businesses through business leagues such as Chambers of Commerce or Realtor's Associations. Businesses experiencing difficulty finding employees benefit from organizations such as the one I am associated with. But another factor is the economic impact of the organizations, for they are businesses themselves. According to the U.S. Bureau of Labor Statistics (BLS), in 2016, nonprofits employed 12.3 million people, or 10.2% of all private sector jobs (TED: The Economics Daily). At the onset of COVID in 2020, 1.6 million nonprofit jobs were lost between March and May of that year. Yet, at that point, they still accounted for 12.4 million jobs representing 14% of the private sector workforce. Between 2007 and 2017, nonprofit job creation was three times greater than for-profit job creation. In 2017, nonprofits represented the third largest payroll, behind only manufacturing and professional services (Nonprofit Hiring Trends and The National Nonprofit Employment Market, 2021). What would be the impact on your community if more than 10% of the jobs suddenly went away?

Charitable nonprofits allow people the opportunity to experience feelings of self-worth, compassion, and joy by helping others. They can be stepping stones to civic engagement and leadership, learning a new skill, or starting a new career. Often, the leaders represent the voice of those they serve.

With strong community relationships and intimate knowledge of the clientele they represent, local nonprofits often understand the best way to meet the needs of the community. They can make our communities safer, healthier, more attractive, and attract new residents and businesses.

But it's a two-way street. Just as the communities depend on the nonprofits, the nonprofits also depend on their communities for support. Many community needs are unmet, and resources are shrinking. Government aid is spread more thinly. Often, support for nonprofits goes to the programs and additional facilities as that's where the need is seen, and what captures the attention of the public and the business community. Contributions may be restricted to use for certain programs and donor-advised funds allow input from the contributor as to where the money can be spent. These are not always the wisest decisions.

The perception has long been that nonprofits that spend the greatest percentage of their funds on expenses related to their stated mission and the programs to enable those missions are the best, most deserving organizations.

Charity Navigator, itself a nonprofit, is an organization that touts itself as 'the world's largest and most trusted nonprofit evaluator. Its role is to gather data on nonprofits, use metrics to evaluate them, and disseminate that information to whoever needs it. The website also states it informs contributors and social investors about how effectively they believe the organization will use funding, how well it has sustained its services over time, and perhaps most importantly, their commitment to best practices, good governance, and transparency (About Us, 2022). However, it was once a perpetrator of the belief that almost every dollar should be spent on programs and that overhead costs for administration and fundraising were bad.

In 2013, the CEOs of Charity Navigator, GuideStar (now Candid GuideStar), and the BBB Wise Giving Alliance gathered and wrote a letter addressing what they called 'The Overhead Myth'. Essentially it said that nonprofits also need governance, leadership, and transparency (Ken Berger, 2013). The response was powerful. Over the next year, more than 100 articles were written on the subject. A second letter was sent out in 2014, and the three organizations, in conjunction with other national organizations such as the National Council of Nonprofits, combined to produce and make available tools and resources to help guide nonprofits to better understand overhead costs (Harold, 2014). Those overhead costs include the evaluation of programs, policies, staff, and leadership. There are costs associated with hiring and retaining qualified people, such as board members, staff, and volunteers. There are also internal systems, such as controls so that funds are not misappropriated, or security breaches are prevented. And, if the costs of fundraising are bad, how is the organization supposed to continue to bring in support? This doesn't mean that excessive overhead costs shouldn't be prevented, but rather that those costs have their place and are a vital factor in the health and longevity of an organization. Note the part about 'best practices, good governance, and transparency, now posted on the Charity Navigator website. Unfortunately, this practice still happens today. Fundraisers, donors, trade associations, and even some charities cling to the belief that overhead is a dirty word. Often, overhead expenses are simply misunderstood (Styron, 2021). For instance, people may believe that all rent expense is overhead, but a portion of that may be related to services provided, such as kennels at an animal shelter.

Imagine a city spending all its money on parks and statues to make itself look good. But no money is spent on the upkeep of roads, or emergency services, utility infrastructure, or maintenance of the parks and statues. How long would this town continue to be a viable community, able to care for its citizens and showcase the beauty it spent so much on? If nonprofits don't train staff, how will they know what to do, and be efficient in doing it? If there is no fundraising, how do they generate funds? If there is no oversight, how would they even know when resources disappear, let alone prevent it from happening? The list goes on.

Nonprofits need communities to support them as much as they support the community. They need places to hold fundraising events, people outside the organization to donate time and services, and for the community to support them in word as well as resources, through media, advertising, and support of politicians, business people, and community leaders. They may need skills-based volunteerism, not just bodies. Don't wait for these organizations to come find you. Instead, learn about the organizations in your community and explore how you can help them help your community.

Community partnerships and joint planning help both the community and the nonprofit. A community government looking to renovate a run-down area may want to consider including nonprofits involved in dealing with animal shelters and homeless shelters in the discussions. This allows for the pre-planning of displaced homeless people and animals who have been seeking refuge in that area. A business looking to enter or expand in that market may be enticed by knowing there is a ready labor force that has been trained by or otherwise assisted by nonprofits. The nonprofit I currently am involved with had a for-profit business staffed in part by those they serve; it was a good community partnership. As Scout leaders, our Scouts often do projects or service work for other area nonprofits. We have collected food donations for a food pantry, installed benches and signs at parks, cleared brush, and built an outdoor meeting place with a fire pit at a Catholic spiritual life center.

A great example of a partnership in my community is the one between a suicide prevention organization and a Harley-Davidson dealership. Every year the nonprofit hosts a fish fry to raise funds. Area businesses sell products for the event or donate supplies and or services in return for recognition of their businesses. The Harley dealership offers its location to hold the event, bringing in a lot of people who would not otherwise visit them. This generates visibility and sales for them. The event is promoted heavily by a local radio station and social media. Volunteers get the benefit of knowing they helped a worthwhile cause.

Communities can support nonprofits, in turn helping the communities, through actively engaging with them, making connections and introductions, serving on their boards, including them in planning sessions, and communicating to the public at large about the benefits the organization brings to the community. The failure of a nonprofit is a failure to its clients, donors, and the community.

The 990 addresses some of this through the telling of the nonprofits' story, and questions revolving around partnerships with businesses and other nonprofits, as well as related business activities between board members and the business with which they are involved.

Traditionally we think of communities as physical locations where we live and work. But there are online communities as well. These communities provide a vital role in times of natural disasters or pandemics, when people are shut in for health reasons, or when divided by great distances. Some are social networking communities such as Facebook or LinkedIn; others may be organizations or chatrooms. Some go beyond this, such as online professional groups or associations. These virtual third communities are alluring because they allow people something different than home or work, where they can meet new people with similar interests and different points of view or with helpful knowledge to impart. Your organization can help foster online communities by having forums on your webpage that foster discussion or hold virtual meetings to provide updates and organize activities.

You can help to empower your supporters online, in turn benefiting your organization. They can share fundraisers online through social media. If they run a business, they could be a supporter of your nonprofit and set up their own online donation page with the funds going to the charity.

Finally, the role of the nonprofit in the community is to benefit those they serve. Sometimes this is obvious and sometimes not. Feeding and sheltering the homeless, providing a home for orphans, youth organizations that build character, and sports leagues are all obvious. A not-so-obvious example is an animal shelter that takes stray animals off the streets that may otherwise pose health and safety risks to people. Then people adopt animals for a reasonable cost instead of paying larger amounts to pet stores or puppy mills. There are those that will still buy from them because they can afford to or want a specific breed of pet. Anywhere there is an unmet need there is an opportunity for an organization to resolve i

Chapter 6

Contributions and Contributors

The role of the contributor is to provide the organization with needed resources. Contributions can take many shapes: time and services, cash, supplies, art, land and buildings, automobiles, boats, aircraft, and other tangible objects. Some cash may be immediate, some may be future pledges, and some may have restrictions as to its use. Unpaid board members, officers, staff, and other volunteers are all contributors of time. The nurse, lawyer, plumber, and others all volunteer not only their time but their expertise.

The impact of these contributions to nonprofits may seem obvious, but there can be caveats. An animal shelter may need funding for pet food and veterinary services, but a contribution may come with the restriction that it be used to build additional kennels. Or the donor may stipulate that they be involved in decisions on how to spend the money. And what about donations from controversial sources? If a dictator from another country, or a convicted murderer, wanted to contribute a large amount of money or resources, how would that look to your other contributors, your staff and volunteers, and the media? Could your organization withstand that kind of scrutiny, and how would it respond? People have to trust you, have faith in you, and once that trust is broken it can be hard to regain, You have to get ahead of it from the start.

A thoughtful and compelling response may change the minds of the naysayers. It could be argued that the benefits of the contribution outweigh the evil of the source. It could also be argued that it is better to accept the money and do good with it than to allow the contributor to spend it on another yacht, mansion, or worse. Mother Teresa is one who felt this way and wasn't afraid to accept such contributions (Joan Harrington, 2020). But the board has to have the insight and fortitude to make these decisions after careful deliberation and choose to reject such contributions or present them in the best light possible if accepted. In cases like this, having a formal policy on accepting contributions is imperative.

Contributions come from many sources and for many reasons. Some nonprofits require their board members to either contribute a set amount or fund raise an equivalent amount, each year. Those involved with religious organizations may follow the custom of 10% tithing and return that amount of their earnings to the organization.

Federated Campaigns were once very popular and are still relevant. These are annual contribution campaigns arranged by other organizations to collect donations and then apportion those contributions among other nonprofits. The campaigns are largely conducted through workplace giving. Probably the most notable example is the United Way. Contributions received as a result of federated campaigns are reported on a separate line on the 990. Often the giving options are organized by a charitable cause or issue. Recipients of federated campaigns tend to be larger, well-established nonprofits. However, smaller and or newer organizations can also be approved depending on the needs fulfilled by the entity. Regardless of the size and tenure of the organization, its financial and governance practices will need to be exemplary to be considered (Monson-Rosen, 2019).

The Combined Federated Campaign (CFC) is overseen by the Office of Personnel Management (OPM) for federal employees and retirees. It is the world's largest annual workplace charitable giving campaign and through 2021 had raised over $8 billion since its inception in 1962.

In 2022 a special CFC campaign was announced in support of Ukraine.

Some businesses run their own workplace campaigns, choosing to support a charity or charities, decided upon by ownership, staff, or a combination of both. This is known as cause marketing. Studies have shown that approximately 90% of consumers are willing to switch brands to one supporting a favorable charity assuming the product or service is similar. Such campaigns can also build employee morale and engagement (Pennel, 2022).

Many associations are nonprofit 501(c)(6) organizations with members. These members will pay dues and may wish to know how those dues are being spent. Often, these organizations will provide members with annual reports, but the 990 may provide additional information. The dues to these organizations are generally not deductible. 501(c)(3) organizations may also have dues (museums, youth organizations, et cetera) and again, the dues are generally not deductible. Of course, there are exceptions. A more specific rule is that the dues are deductible to the extent the dues exceed the value of benefits received. In some cases, the organization may be required to inform the members in writing as to what is or is not deductible (Are Membership Dues Tax-Deductible?, ND).

Church tithing is a form of contributing. Donors support the church but often the church sponsors related charities or programs. The church may charter Scout Troops or provide a meeting place for your garden club or book club. It may support work camps, orphanages, or food banks. Parishioners may contribute directly to some of these other organizations, or just to the church with the understanding that a percentage of those funds will be spent on programs in keeping with the faith.

Grants are a form of contribution generally provided by corporations, foundations, or governments.

Corporations will give grants to charities because it can benefit them as well as the recipient organization, and hence that organization's recipients. It builds a positive public image of the company. In a poll conducted for Fortune, millennials are more likely than others to buy from and work for businesses that support charitable causes (Notte, 2018). It can also improve workplace performance as feeling positive about the culture of the company and workplace volunteering have been shown to increase happiness and productivity in employees. Corporate–nonprofit partnerships can be beneficial to both organizations and not just in the sense of the corporation 'looking good.' For instance, the British nonprofit Campaign Against Living Miserably is a mental health and suicide prevention organization that offers mental health training to staff at corporate sponsors.

Whereas nonprofits get their funding through sources such as public donations, fundraisers, program service fees, and grants, private foundations get their funding from one source: an individual, family, or corporation. This allows them control of the mission, who is on the board, and how and where funds are invested. Some nonprofits, especially smaller ones, may be chagrined to learn that a publicly funded nonprofit cannot have most of its board comprised of people related by blood or marriage (What is a Private Foundation?, ND).

On average, nonprofits receive about one-third of their funding through government grants. Governments give these grants because nonprofits can provide services more effectively and cost-efficiently than governments can provide those same services to the public. Nonprofit groups and government offices have also been working together in recent years to improve collaborative efforts. For instance, the National Council of Nonprofits and the Office of Management and Budget have worked to better government-nonprofit relationships and grant/contracting systems (Government Grants/Contracting, ND).

Individuals may contribute cash, stock donations, non-cash supplies, or time and services. As a volunteer with the Society of St. Andrew, I spent two or more hours once a week gleaning fruits and vegetables (time). I would also organize groups and show new participants what to do and deliver produce to food banks (services and time). I got fresh air and exercise, met new people, and got a great sense of well-being from helping others. Cash contributions may be restricted or unrestricted. Restricted means the funds must be earmarked and used for certain purposes such as particular programs. Freedom Alliance is a Northern Virginia nonprofit that runs several programs benefiting wounded veterans and the families of wounded or deceased veterans. One of these is a program that awards scholarships to the children of veterans to help them pay for college. If somebody contributes and indicates that the funds are for scholarships, then those funds are restricted to use only for that program. In this way, people can support things that are meaningful to them.

People want to feel good about themselves; they want to make a difference. As an added incentive, they get tax deductions for cash and non-cash donations, though a donation of time is not deductible. They may not need an added incentive, but sometimes it's there. A volunteer helping with an event, a sponsor of that event, or the contributor who gets tickets to the event in partial exchange for the contribution, may partake in something that otherwise wouldn't be possible for them. It could be that they get to attend a concert by their favorite performer, meet their favorite celebrity, or get a meal from the top restaurant in town.

This brings us to another point. Volunteers and contributors should be acknowledged. Not just because it's the right thing to do, but in the case of cash contributions it may be required. If a donor writes your organization a check of $250 or more, you are required to send them a confirmation of that contribution no later than the individual tax filing deadline for that tax year. Under IRS Sect 513(h)(2), for donations in excess of $75 that contain a 'quid pro quo' valuation, the nonprofit must notify the contributor of the amount of that contribution that is not deductible. To put this plainly, a nonprofit holds a fundraising event featuring a concert performed by a band that usually sells concert tickets for $40 each. The person attending the event pays $100 to get in. the nonprofit must acknowledge the $100 and also state that the value of the ticket is non-deductible. If the value of the event or item received is minimal then the full amount is deductible. For 2022, that amount is $11.70; it is inflation adjusted each year. The taxpayer will need the acknowledgments if ever audited, and the nonprofit can be assessed penalties for not providing them (Substantiating Charitable Contributions, ND).

Chapter 7

Monitoring

Many different individuals, governments, and organizations may monitor your nonprofit in some way. Their reasoning may be regulatory such as conducted by the IRS or the state(s) in which you conduct activities. It may be the media looking for or following up on a story. Nonprofit rating and/or information-gathering organizations, potential contributors, the media, and others all could be interested in your organization for differing reasons and could examine the 990, annual report, website, or other available information. The purpose of these investigations can be for compliance, improvement, inquisitive, or even sinister.

The most important, and most effective, monitoring is for your nonprofit to conduct self-assessments. Doing so could detect any issues more rapidly, leading to resolutions to any potential problems. This is preferable to having someone else discover issues and possibly having them dragged through the media. Self-assessments can be conducted either organization-wide or by focusing on specific areas such as the progress of certain programs, fundraising effectiveness, board participation, or gaps in the training of staff or volunteers.

These assessments usually occur annually and may coincide with an upcoming audit. But that does not mean that internal monitoring should be limited to an annual procedure. They should be designed to help boards and staff more rapidly identify areas for improvement and strengthen future performance. Examples are making certain conflict-of-interest policies are being followed, accounts are being reconciled regularly, and that the organization is still true to its stated mission.

Internal monitoring should also include keeping abreast of changes that can impact the organization, whether regulatory, community based, economic or environmental. Being aware of changes in laws affecting nonprofits is imperative to avoid penalties or possible loss of exempt status. Shifting demographics in the community can impact the organizations' revenues and effectiveness. Recent economic turmoil resulted in declining contributions. A tax law change for 2020 and 2021 allowed for a tax deduction for charitable contributions even for those who do not itemize on their returns. Did your organization promote this as an incentive for people to contribute? Being aware of projected weather patterns could help with planning for organizations dependent on outdoor activities.

Outside businesses may review your 990 to see if your organization is a potential business client. Auditors and tax professionals are obvious examples of ones who may do this. But consider that a properly prepared 990 will contain information about business dealings between the organization and any officers, directors, key employees, or family members of any of them. These dealings are potential sources of revenue for other business owners, especially if there is a change in the organization's officers, directors, or key personnel.

There are many people and companies who may want to do business with your organization. Some businesses specialize in working with nonprofits. An insurance agent may look at the amount of insurance expense listed on the 990. I know one who specializes in insurance policies for nonprofits.

I know another businessman who works closely with nonprofits on website design, social media presence, and event marketing. He can easily look to see how your organization is portrayed online. This could lead him to contact you to offer assistance in making improvements.

Other nonprofits may review your 990 to discover any potential synergy between the two organizations that they might wish to explore. People considering starting a nonprofit may look at the 990 to get an idea of what your organization does to see if it meets the needs of its intended recipients. They may also look to see what compensation officers or board members receive, or who is on the board of directors.

Then there are nonprofits that provide information and rankings on other nonprofits. The two primary ones have already been mentioned: Charity Navigator and Candid GuideStar. Both provide copies of all 990s. They also rank nonprofits on various metrics such as financial health, governance, and transparency. All nonprofits have the potential to be ranked on Candid GuideStar based on the information they request from, or is supplied by, the organization. Charity Navigator is much more limited, ranking only those organizations that meet certain qualifications including that it must be a 501(c)(3), have annual revenue of at least $1 million in the preceding two years, and have been in operation for at least seven years. Great Nonprofits also provides 990s on their website and offers a ranking of sorts known as the Top-Rated Award. This is awarded when any donor, supporter, client, or volunteer nominates that nonprofit with a 4 or 5-star rating.

These organizations cull the 990s from the IRS Exempt-Organization page. IRS delays from COVID have affected the processing of 990s just like every other type of return, especially those that were paper filed before that process became no longer acceptable. It is not unusual to search for a 990 for a charity only to find that 2018 or 2019 are the most recent that are available. Candid

GuideStar uses the information to flow into their FDO Foundation Directory tool that grant makers utilize. Working with data two years old or older isn't very effective. And the trend in processing times was already getting worse pre-COVID. While it is not the only source, the IRS is a vital one (Koob, 2021).

Grantors such as supporting organizations like United Way or Giving Forward will review your 990. Private foundations, and local, state, or federal governments will review information available on your financial strength, adherence to your mission, board engagement, and good governance practices among other things. This may be found in your 990, annual report, audit, or other locations.

The IRS says that Federal law does not generally mandate particular policies or practices listed in Section A. Also, the policies and procedures asked about in Section B are generally not required under the IRC. The IRS also says that, while not necessarily required, having many of these policies in place is good governance and promotes tax compliance. The 990 instructions state that failure to have such policies can lead to activities inconsistent with tax-exempt statuses, such as transactions that excessively benefit individuals within the organization rather than those intended to benefit from the donated or granted funds.

Regardless of the type of entity, or whether the policies are in place, all organizations filing a full 990 are required to answer each of the questions in Part V. Further, contrary to the IRS assertion that the policies are not required, some are. Although the Sarbanes-Oxley Act (SOX) generally applies to public corporations, two provisions also apply to nonprofits: provisions prohibiting retaliation against whistle-blowers and prohibiting the destruction, alteration, or concealment of certain documents or the impediment of an investigation into such actions. Conflict-of-Interest policies, though not mandated, are one of the primary policies the IRS looks for. Unmanaged conflicts resulting in excess benefits can result in intermediate sanctions (significant penalties) against both the individual(s) who derive any benefits, as well as the organization.

There are other regulations the IRS will look at, and failure to abide by them can result in severe penalties. Previously discussed was self-inurement, but there are others. One example is dealing with blacklisted countries. It is the duty of the nonprofit's leaders to be aware of these rules and follow them.

In 2022 the IRS started self-study classes on nonprofit matters including maintaining 501(c)(3) status, employment issues, unrelated business income, and more. These started coming out in February 2022; the latest as of this writing was a 42-page technical guide (rather than a course) on 501(c)(6) business leagues. These further strengthen the IRS's position on compliance, governance, and transparency.

States may require and review 990s along with other annual filings. For example, Virginia requires either a one-time or an annual charitable solicitation filing, depending on the extent of the solicitations. Any nonprofit required to file a 990-T with the IRS is required to file Virginia's Form 500 (except nonprofit hospitals). Another would be New York, which requires a Form CHAR500 from all charities operating in the state, which includes attaching the 990 with all schedules excerpt Schedule B. Also, states may require is a review or audit report depending on revenues or the dollar amount of state grants. New York, for example, requires a review if revenues are greater than $250,000 up to $1,000,000, and an audit report if revenues are in excess of $1,000,000 (Segal, 2022). It's possible your organization may not be aware of the requirement, but when the states review the 990, they will certainly make you aware of it.

Contributors, whether governments or granting organizations, the general public, other nonprofit organizations, employees, or volunteers of the organization, will want to see how the money they infuse into the entity is utilized. They may look at factors such as how many clients are helped, the percentage of funds spent on management expenses, or if a large portion of funds is spent on officer salaries and employee benefits. They may assess if the organization is financially stable: by looking at its assets and if revenues outpacing expenses. Does the 990 reflect the organization's public image? In other words, a nonprofit that says it's a grassroots organization should show a lot of volunteers, and one that professes to spend a certain percentage on program expenses better reflect that on the 990. How does it derive its revenues and is it sustainable? Are revenues consistent, growing, or declining? The first page offers a two-year comparison.

The media may review the 990, looking for details when covering a story about the organization's activities and events, background on either positive or negative stories, or information as background on an officer or director.

Employees may want additional information including officer compensation, areas of the organization they may not be aware of, or more worrisome to the organization, things they may be aware of and are looking to see if it's being adequately reported. A disgruntled employee, or former employee, could potentially bring about negative publicity if they see something they know to be inaccurate. All the more reason to properly disclose information on an accurate, well-presented 990.

Volunteers, whether current, past or present, may want to review the 990 to learn more about the organization. Potential volunteers may look at the organization's mission, what impact the organization has had on those they serve (assuming the organization provides this information on the 990), the governance of the organization, and those that serve as officers and directors.

Advisors may review your 990 to market their services to you if paid, or to see if their goals and values align with those of your organization before accepting a request to be a volunteer advisor.

There are other reasons someone may want to review the 990 such as personal, political, or religious. I worked for a firm that prepared the annual 990 for an organization that reported on climate change. One day someone called the firm and asked to speak with the preparer of the 990. They asked for information on those offering business services to the organization, and those making contributions. Both requests were denied. While most 501(c)(3) organizations are required to report information to the IRS on those who contribute over a certain amount, this is the one piece of information from the 990 that does not get shared with the public. This person was someone who disagreed with the nonprofit's mission and was looking to stir up trouble. Be honest and informative with your 990 but be aware that there are those who may look for things for reasons that do not benefit the organization.

Chapter 8

Closing Comments

This book is far from comprehensive. Much more detail and guidance can be given on what has been covered, and there are topics not covered at all. The idea was to give you some basics and inform you of things you may not have been aware of or given much consideration to in the past. It is up to you to utilize what you learn and be willing to improve your organization and its image. Some things are required by regulation, but many are not. There's nothing that says you can't pay your officers and employees reasonable salaries, but what is reasonable? If those salaries comprise 80% of the expenses, there are many who would question it. But if there's a legitimate purpose, such as it being a nonprofit emergency clinic, then that may be more reasonable. How you spend your revenues, and how you paint your picture, is up to you. But the more successful nonprofits will take advantage of every bit of knowledge available that they are aware of.

Advisors, consultants, contributors, employees, and volunteers are all resources, but there is other help to be found. Astute board members, officers, and staff may be aware of some and may find other sources. A good advisor or consultant can assist with locating and utilizing others. One resource that many nonprofits don't utilize is networking groups. I have belonged to four different ones over the past half-dozen years and only one had any nonprofit participation at all. In that group, the nonprofit was absent more often than not. Yet, the networking group had as members business owners who had expertise in their fields that related to nonprofits.

Many nonprofit organizations have other nonprofit organizations as their members. These exist to provide and share information with the member organizations, gather information from those organizations to lobby on nonprofit issues, and discover what issues they are facing so they may address them. On the national level, there is the National Council of Nonprofits, among others. This organization has chapters in nearly every state. There can also be organizations on a regional or local basis. Many local cooperatives are under the auspices of the Chamber of Commerce in those communities.

Do you think you would like to start a nonprofit? Maybe you've identified a need, or what you believe to be an under-served need, in your community. Or maybe you have a pet project, such as rescuing exotic pets turned loose in the wild. There are many factors to consider when starting your own nonprofit. Some should be accounted for prior to initiating the process of starting one. Where will the initial funding come from to get it started? How will you market it to potential donors; convincing them of the need for the organization and why they should support this one? Is it relevant? Does it overlap the services of existing organizations in the area? If so, you may want to consider joining them instead of competing for the same funding, unless the need is great enough to call for both organizations.

As my family once lost our home to a fire and I saw firsthand how it affected each of us, my dream is to someday start a nonprofit that benefits those displaced by fires. My focus would be my community and possibly nearby communities as well. Sadly, many people are displaced each year in my community by fires. This demonstrates a real need for such an organization. In Ohio, where tornadoes are a common occurrence, someone may consider opening an organization to assist those affected by them. But would there be a similar need in San Diego, California? Currently, the last tornado to hit San Diego County occurred in 2007, and there have been only 17 tornadoes reported there since 1950 (Tornado Information for San Diego, California, ND). Or one day you see a baby kangaroo near your home and want to start that exotic pet rescue. While ownership of exotic pets in the U.S. is growing and now represents a 15-billion-dollar industry, only 1,300 such animals were reported to have escaped into the wild between 1990 and 2021 (Miles, 2022). Unless your organization offered services to help track down these animals nationwide, there wouldn't be much of a need for your organization to exist.

As you think about starting a nonprofit consider the questions in the first paragraph of this chapter: is there a need, where is the initial funding coming from, will you be fighting for the same funding as another organization, how will the organization be classed (3, 4, 6, or another), and who will be the initial leaders? Make certain you understand the processes of setting it up and get professional assistance if there is any doubt. Be sure to have well-stated procedures and controls in place from the start. It will be your duty to do right by those who work with you, those who provide you with funding, and those to whom you offer assistance.

I will reiterate the value of a properly prepared 990. You must have someone with intricate knowledge of the forms and regulations, and you should have a good understanding as well. The instructions are more than 100 pages and are updated annually, and the IRS says they are not official guidance that can be cited in defense of a position. Throughout the instructions, it references Internal Revenue Code Sections and regulations. This means the actual instructions, once researched further, are even more complex. I take continuing education every year concerning at least a few areas of the 990. Courses on just a single section or schedule can take hours to complete. It is your role to make certain the rules are being followed and that a qualified preparer is utilized, while the role of the IRS is to monitor, and the preparer's role is to present the 990 in the best possible light without any inaccuracy or falsity.

Nonprofits play a pivotal role in their community by way of providing employment and learning opportunities, services to individuals and the community at large, as well as collaboration with businesses. Businesses, volunteers, contributors, and others have a role to play in the nonprofit organization. Each may have a defined title, role, or even written policies and descriptions of duties and expectations. Ultimately it is the actions of each that truly defines their role. One may have the best-defined opportunity, but if they do not take action, or take inappropriate action, they will take on the role of a laggard, or worse, an embezzler, scam artist, or whatever moniker is bestowed upon them by those affected. And, though someone of good character can become an exemplary role model without perfect guidance, it shouldn't be left to chance.

Bibliography

About Us. (2022). Retrieved October 2, 2022, from Charity Navigator: https://www.charitynavigator.org/index.cfm?bay=content.view&cpid=8658

Are Membership Dues Tax-Deductible? (ND). Retrieved August 31, 2022, from Network for Good: https://www.networkforgood.com/resource/are-membership-dues-tax-deductible/

Bryce, H. J. (2017, August 21). *Nonprofit Board Responsibilities: The Basics.* Retrieved from Nonprofit Quarterly: https://nonprofitquarterly.org/nonprofit-board-governance-responsibilities-basic-guide/rofiy

DiPaulo, G. (2019, March 27). *UP students dress as princesses and superheroes to bring magic to children's hospitals.* Retrieved from The Beacon: https://www.upbeacon.com/article/2019/03/a-moment-of-magic-students-dress-as-princesses-and-superheroes

Divirgilio, D. (2015, February 26). *Is My Church a Nonprofit?* Retrieved from Faith Based Nonprofit Resource Center: https://non-profitconsultant.com/church-nonprofit/#:~:text=The%20short%20answer%20is%20no.%20Churches%2C%20by%20definition%2C,become%20a%20registered%20501%20%28c%29%20%283%29%20nonprofit%20organization.

Ensor, K. (2022, September 13). *A Complete List of Types of Nonprofits: Which One Should You Start?* Retrieved from Donorbox Blog: https://donorbox.org/nonprofit-blog/types-of-nonprofits

Fortenberry, J. (2022). *The Inurement Prohibition & Non-Profit Organizations.* Retrieved October 1, 2022, from Fortenberry Law: https://www.fortenberrylaw.com/inurement-prohibition-nonprofit-organizations/

Government Grants/Contracting. (ND). Retrieved September 15,

2022, from National Council of Nonprofits: https://www.councilofnonprofits.org/trends-policy-issues/government-grants-contracting

GUIDEBOOK FOR NEW HAMPSHIRE CHARITABLE ORGANIZATIONS. (2022, February). Retrieved October 2, 2022, from Department of Justice - New Hampshire: chrome-extension://efaidnbmnnnibpcajpcglclefindmkaj/https://www.doj.nh.gov/charitable-trusts/documents/guidebook-non-profit-organizations.pdf

Harold, J. (2014, October 31). *Moving From the Overhead Myth to an Overhead Solution: Next Steps.* Retrieved from Philanthropy News Digest: https://philanthropynewsdigest.org/features/commentary-and-opinion/moving-from-the-overhead-myth-to-an-overhead-solution-next-steps

Joan Harrington, A. V. (2020, September 23). *Controversial Donors: A Guide to Ethical Gift Acceptance for Nonprofit Organizations.* Retrieved from Markkula Center for Applied Ethics: https://www.scu.edu/ethics/ethical-gift-acceptance/guide-to-ethical-gift-acceptance/controversial-donors-a-guide-to-ethical-gift-acceptance-for-nonprofit-organizations.html

Ken Berger, J. H. (2013, June 17). *Nonprofit Quarterly.* Retrieved from The Overhead Myth: https://nonprofitquarterly.org/the-overhead-myth/

Koob, A. (2021, May 12). *Where are the 2019 (and 2020) 990s? On filling the gaps in Candid's grants data.* Retrieved from Candid: https://blog.candid.org/post/where-are-the-2019-and-2020-990s-on-filling-the-gaps-in-candids-grants-data/

Michael I Sanders, &. N. (2017, April 23). *United States: Congressional Response To The Smithsonian Institution And Allegations Of Abuse: What Could It Mean For Other Nonprofit Organizations?* Retrieved from mondaq: https://www.mondaq.com/unitedstates/tax-authorities/47876/congressional-response-to-the-smithsonian-institution-and-allegations-of-abuse-what-could-it-mean-for-other-nonprofit-organizations

Miles, E. (2022, January 22). *Latest Exotic Pet Statistics in 2022 [Ownership & Attacks].* Retrieved from Pawsome Advice: https://pawsomeadvice.com/pets/exotic-pet-statistics/

Monson-Rosen, M. (2019, June 6). *Federated Funds for US Nonprofits: What Are They and Who's Eligible?* Retrieved from Mission Box Global Network> US: https://www.missionbox.com/article/35/federated-funds-for-us-nonprofits-what-are-they-and-whos-eligible

Nonprofit Hiring Trends and The National Nonprofit Employment Market. (2021, July 8). Retrieved from Foundation list: https://www.foundationlist.org/nonprofit-hiring-trends-and-the-national-nonprofit-employment-market/

Notte, J. (2018, January 25). Retrieved from The Street: https://www.thestreet.com/lifestyle/why-millennials-are-more-charitable-14445741

Pennel, L. (2022, September 21). *Workplace Giving 101: The Impact of Workplace Giving Campaigns.* Retrieved from Global Impact: https://charity.org/give-global-blog/workplace-giving-101/

Pikora, J. (2022, June 29). *Christian Theatre Director In Central PA Assaulted Four Girls He Plied With Alcohol: Police.* Retrieved from Daily Voice: https://dailyvoice.com/pennsylvania/dauphin/news/christian-theatre-director-in-central-pa-assaulted-four-girls-he-plied-with-alcohol-police/836447/

State Filing Requirements for Nonprofits. (2022). Retrieved October 1, 2022, from National Council of Nonprofits: https://www.councilofnonprofits.org/tools-resources/state-filing-requirements-nonprofits

Styron, L. (2021, October 21). *Busting the Myths of "The*

Overhead Myth". Retrieved from Charity Watch: https://www.charitywatch.org/charity-donating-articles/busting-the-myths-of-the-overhead-myth

Substantiating Charitable Contributions. (ND). Retrieved July 17, 2021, from IRS: https://www.irs.gov/charities-non-profits/substantiating-charitable-contributions

TED: The Economics Daily. (n.d.). Retrieved October 2, 2022, from U.S. Bureau of Labor Statistics: https://www.bls.gov/opub/ted/2018/nonprofits-account-for-12-3-million-jobs-10-2-percent-of-private-sector-employment-in-2016.htm

Tornado Information for San Diego, California. (ND). Retrieved October 2, 2022, from Home Facts: https://www.homefacts.com/tornadoes/California/San-Diego-County/San-Diego.html

What is a Private Foundation? (ND). Retrieved October 2, 2022, from Foundation Source: https://foundationsource.com/what-is-a-private-foundation/

Wyland, M. (2018, July 17). *How Many Nonprofits Are There?: What the IRS's Nonprofit Automatic Revocation and 1023-EZ Processes Left Behind.* Retrieved from Nonprofit Quarterly: https://nonprofitquarterly.org/how-many-nonprofits-1023ez/

Zagorsky, J. (2015, May 4). *Why the NFL and other professional sports don't deserve nonprofit status.* Retrieved from The Ohio State University Jay Zagorsky's Research & Blog: https://u.osu.edu/zagorsky.1/2015/05/04/nfl-2/

www.ingramcontent.com/pod-product-compliance
Lightning Source LLC
Chambersburg PA
CBHW071348290326
41933CB00041B/3051

* 9 7 9 8 2 1 8 0 8 7 8 7 6 *